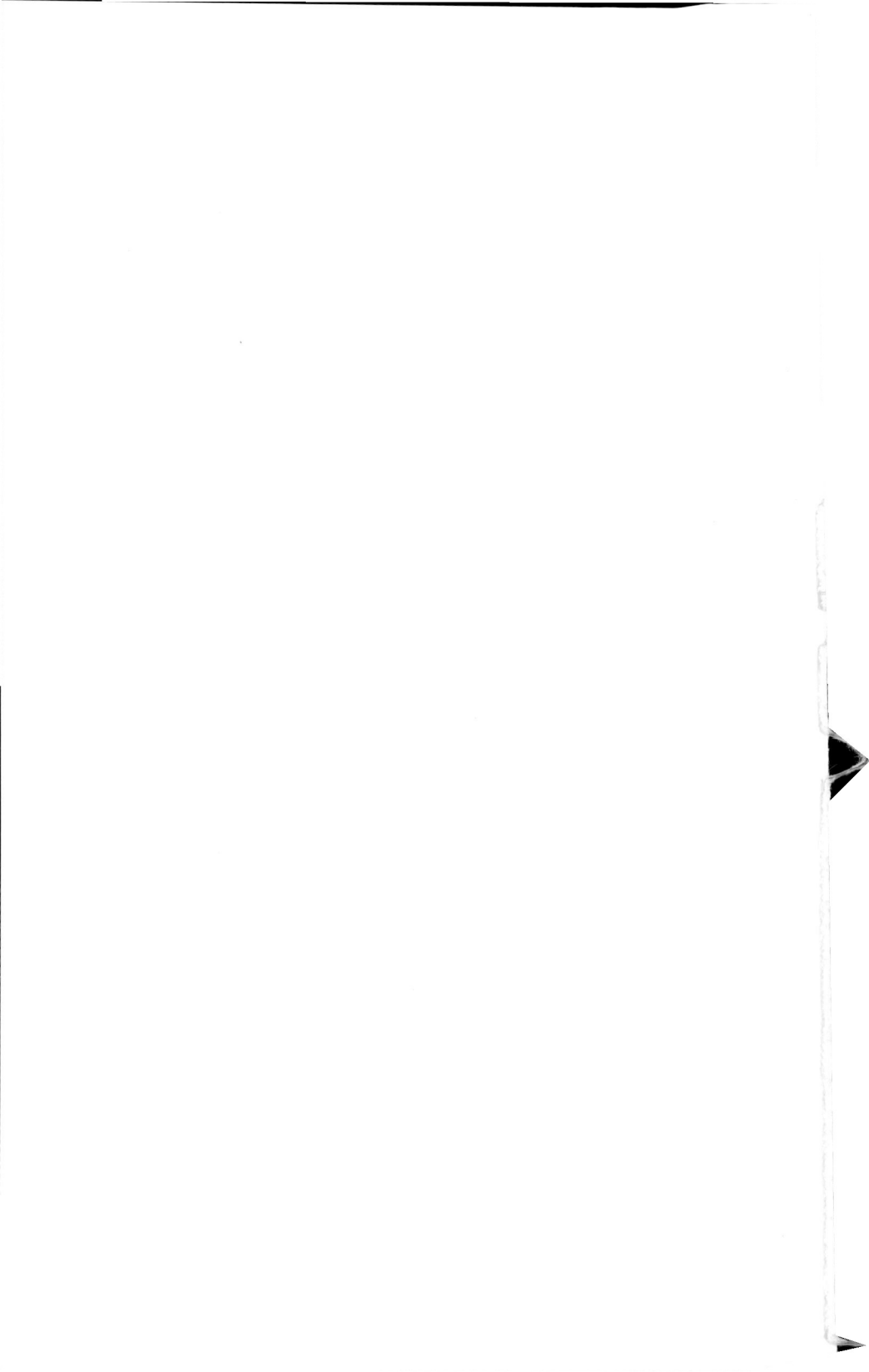

Before you take the 1 Hour Prayer Challenge, if you have never accepted Jesus Christ as your personal Lord and Savior, you can pray the salvation prayer and get saved right now.

SALVATION PRAYER

God, I openly confess and declare with my mouth that Jesus is Lord, and believe in my heart that God raised him from the dead.

When you pray that prayer, according to Romans 10:9, you are saved. Get connected with a good, bible-based church in your area to continue your new life with Jesus.

I am so excited for you! Feel free to email me and let me know that you accepted Jesus Christ as your personal Lord and Savior. I can be reached at info@onassignmentbyGod.com

Contents

CAN I TESTIFY?

The week of February 18, 2019 changed my life forever.

But let's go back to 2018 so you can see exactly how I arrived into this life changing week.

Let's take a journey together, okay? Alright, let's go!

2018

I had been in an ungodly soultie. This relationship that I was in where I thought I was so in love, was finally coming to a screeching halt. It had already been tumultuous and I had been hurt so many times. God was chasing after me in a major way and I was trying to handle it all on my own. I was trying to use what I knew. I was thinking, if I could just show them how loyal I am. If I could just show them how faithful I am. If I could just show them...wait, them? God was saying, you are so busy trying to show this person who has been totally unfaithful to you what faithful looks like, that you're totally missing that I AM the only one who can show you what a faithful love that endures forever looks like, feels like, is like. I AM the only one who can show you an unfailing love. This guy has already failed you numerous times.

I knew that too. Buuuuuut I kept saying....

If he could just see that I am worthy.

If he could just see how loyal I am.

If he could just see how forgiving I am.

If he could just see how faithful I am.

If he could just see how dedicated I am.

If he could just see that I was worth it.

2018 was the year where the Lord had had enough. He was saying the same thing to me that I was saying to him!

If she could just see that I am worthy of all her praise.

If she could just see how loyal I am to my creations.

If she could just see how forgiving I am and what I did for her on the cross.

If she could just see how my faithful love endures forever.

If she could just see how dedicated I am to her destiny.

If she could just see the worth that I placed on the inside of her for MY GLORY.

The Lord was chasing after me. He was letting me find out about every lie. He was showing me everything I needed to know about this person. He kept showing me. Over and over and over and over and over and over and over again.

Now usually it doesn't take me long to learn a lesson, but in this case, it was taking me a while. I had been divorced from my husband of 12 years, with two kids in tow, and I was banking on this investment I had made in this counterfeit stock.

I want to say parenthetically that this person has since made a 180 degree change in their life and God has done a mighty work for both of us. But that only came from a full 100% surrender to God's will.

I remember it like it was yesterday. The Lord was telling me, it's time to cut ties. I didn't want to. I figured the Lord could fix us TOGETHER. He said, "break it off now." I kept putting it off. I wasn't sure how to do it. Things kept happening that was making it worse. The guy kept being exposed with the things he was doing. I was watching videos about men and the games they play because I was always trying to figure it out on my own. But that's not what God wanted me to do. He didn't want me to figure it out. He wanted me to "BREAK IT OFF NOW."

Finally the Lord gave me an ultimatum: Don't go into the New Year with him. Break it off. He told me this like in November, if I recall correctly, and I was still trying to figure out how I was going to break it off. I had forgiven the guy more times than I could count.

The day finally came.

I broke it off.

2019

Happy New Year!!! 2019 came roaring in and I was once again all alone bringing in the New Year. My kids were with their Dad as usual and I was bringing in another year like I had done the last few years. I had no idea what a transformational year this would be, but God did.

During the month of January, we had a guest speaker come to our church by the name of Teri Savelle Foy. She was this petite woman with a very distinctive voice. She had all these goofy little props during her message and I enjoyed her so much that I went to her table after service to buy her 5 *Things Successful People Do Before 8 a.m. Kit.* It had her book of the same title, a dreams and goals journal, a habit tracker, and a few other things.

I remember immediately reading most of the book (but I don't believe I finished it), and making some goals in the journal. I wanted to spend more time with the Lord. I wanted to pay off some debt. I wanted to give $1000. There were a few other goals as well.

Also in the month of January, I would find out from my employer that they wanted to transition me out of the office to do my work from home as a contractor. I would be losing my health benefits, retirement, and I would now be working in isolation.

Side Note: Back in August 2018, my employer decided that I should no longer be the director of a program that I successfully established. But that I should be the marketing team of one instead. At the time it was so crazy to me. I didn't even understand. All I mostly remember from what I believed to be a career shattering day, was emailing my team the Romans 8:28 scripture.

> *We know that God is always at work for the good of everyone who loves him. They are the ones God has chosen for his purpose.*
>
> *Romans 8:28 CEV*

Okay so back to January 2019 where my employer was now making another decision to transition me out of the office into a contract position. The pay would be less. But I have to just give a shout of praise because while my pay was less, I made and kept more money in 2019 than I had ever made. It was a set up. It was a divinely orchestrated set up by God.

I finished up my last day at the office in January and headed into February, now working from home. I had been an entrepreneur prior to this director job, so being back in the work from home environment wasn't new to me.

February comes and I am now working from home. I actually kinda like it. No more acting like I was working when I really wasn't. Now I know what you're probably thinking...you weren't working at the office? Nope, not a whole lot. But I come from the school of MBA, hard knocks, and a resume that starts at the age of 14. I never subscribed to working harder. I have always worked smarter. And still do (smile).

I was now home and getting settled in. My church was kicking off Life Group Season and I was excited to find a group that I could get into. I told this story in my last book, *Permission Slips* (not a shameless plug), but I was NOT looking for a prayer group. I didn't know what I was looking for, but it wasn't a prayer group. I had previously done some life groups where we read books, kind of like a bookclub, so I was always going to be drawn to those. I saw this one group with the title, Queenology, but it was already filled. I was kind of disappointed because it was the author of this book who I had been binge watching YouTube episodes toward the end of 2018 and God was using this man's videos to help me see why I needed to exit that relationship I was in.

I didn't find a Life Group on Connect Night at the church (where we could physically peruse the group tables), but I was determined to get online and find a group. I remember lying on my bed looking at the groups on my phone. The zumba group that I had considered was filled, but the Queenology group now had some openings! I signed up right away and was feeling so good. I couldn't wait to get with other women to talk about the book!

I kept scrolling and I saw this group called the 1 Hour Prayer Challenge. My first thought was, what can you pray about for an hour? But I was super intrigued by the description of the group. Plus it was a group that didn't actually meet in person. I could do the group from my phone. It was a prayer accountability group. Yes! I liked this a whole lot. Plus I remembered my goal of wanting to spend more time with the Lord, so I was like, this may work. I signed up.

Now, what I didn't know a whole lot about was praying in the spirit (or praying in tongues), but the group leader assured me on the phone that I would be fine. She said, just come down front after church to receive prayer for the infilling of the Holy Spirit. There would be prayer team workers at the altar who would be able to assist.

Guess who missed the opportunity to have the prayer team pray over them? Yes, you guessed it! Me!

The 1-Hour Prayer Challenge was starting the next day and I had not received the gift of speaking in tongues! What was I going to do? She assured me that we could try again the next Sunday. The group leader also offered me the opportunity to come to her home as well. So I started the week off praying like I knew to pray. But I was feeling some kind of way that I wasn't going to be with everyone else, even though with this challenge, you were praying on your own, not in a group setting or on a group prayer call.

I prayed Monday for over 15 minutes and was excited that I went over the time.

I prayed Tuesday and journaled.

I prayed Wednesday and the outline of a book (now called *Permission Slips*) just flowed out of me.

I prayed Thursday.

Friday came. I prayed and asked the Lord for the infilling of the Holy Spirit. I started speaking in tongues! Right there in my prayer closet. I couldn't believe it. I actually spoke in my heavenly language for the very first time!!! I was so excited! I wrote it down, February 22, 2019.

But then I started second guessing what had happened. Could I have baptized myself in the Holy Spirit? Nah? What if I didn't do it right? Was it possible to do by yourself without going down to the front of the church for them to lay hands on me in prayer? Did I really receive the Holy Spirit? Did I?

The next day was the first meeting of Queenology bookclub Life Group. I was excited to be meeting with the ladies. I got there and only one car was outside. I was like, now I know this group was full when I signed up, but okay. I went inside the beautiful home of the life group leader and began socializing with the one other guest who was there. She was actually the co-leader of the life group. After a bit of chatting, we realized that it would just be us three for this first meeting.

The ladies and I kept the conversation going and I told them about the other life group I had joined called the 1 Hour Prayer Challenge. Then one of the ladies said something that shocked me completely. She said, "Oh we prayed for a few people in your group at the altar this past Sunday for them to receive the Holy Spirit."

I was floored. My eyes were probably looking like a deer in headlights. These two women were the exact two women who had prayed over the other members in the 1 Hour Prayer Challenge group. These were the very two women whom I had missed my opportunity with on the previous Sunday before the challenge started. Here I was sitting in the home of the prayer team who had prayed. Y'all can't know how excited and overwhelmed I was in that moment. God had done it again. It was a set up. I had told them about my prayer the day before and how I thought I had received the Holy Spirit, but started second guessing myself. And God had divinely orchestrated a private prayer session just for me, with the very women who had prayed for the other members in my group. These two women prayed over me and ensured me that I had indeed already received the Holy Spirit. But the Lord knew his daughter. He knew I needed the official, otherwise I would have always second guessed if I was legit!

15

And from that moment on, my life transformed over the entire year of 2019 like never before.

I met the 1 Hour prayer challenge.

I kept going after the challenge was over and prayed consistently every morning for a total of 316 days!!!!

During that challenge, the Holy Spirit gave me a book during my time with Him one morning. He instructed me to write it in 30 days and I procrastinated and wasn't obedient. Then He told me, you now have 3 days to do it and I want you to fast while you do it. My last book, *Permission Slips*, was written in 3 days while fasting! That still blows my mind!

He told me to start sharing our conversations during March 2019. I asked how? He answered, you already know how. So I started blogging in March 2019. I ended the year with 240 daily blogs. You can find me still blogging My Conversation With God over at On Assignment by God dot com.

To top it all off, the leader of the 1 Hour Prayer Challenge (shout out to Kathy Smith) left the church to return back to her home church, and the Holy Spirit told me to lead the group. At the time of this publishing, I have led this challenge 4 times already and many lives have been transformed just like mine was.

I am super excited for you to have this book (another assignment from the Lord) so that you can do the 1 Hour Prayer Challenge anytime you get ready. You can lead others in the challenge like I have, whether it be in your family, in your church, and even in your friend circles. I will admit, doing the challenge is way more fun when you can have others holding you accountable and encouraging you to the finish.

Without any more delay, let's start the 1 Hour Prayer Challenge!

The Challenge Starts Now!

I want to personally welcome you to the 1 Hour Prayer Challenge! I pray that you will experience the amazing transformation in your prayer life that I received when I was a *participant* in this challenge in February 2019! Let me just say this...taking on this challenge completely changed my entire life and I am not exaggerating one bit! I pray that it has that same POWER for you!

Now bare with me because I know this first group of instructions is kinda long, but I want to make sure you get all you need to succeed in this life-changing challenge!

Now I know you're already asking the very question I asked when I signed up for this challenge. How can I pray for 1 whole hour? Trust me, I know. But believe me when I say, this challenge structure totally helped me reach my goal of spending more time with the Lord. Prayer is how you communicate with God. The challenge is also designed to help you consistently spend quality time praying in the Spirit (your heavenly language). I want to be really transparent in telling you that when I took this challenge, I had not been baptized in the Holy Ghost, or received the gift of the Holy Ghost, which is initially evidenced by speaking with other tongues (Acts 2:4). But before I started the challenge, our group leader at the time, encouraged us to visit the prayer team after church service, but I missed it. So one morning, during my first week of the challenge, I decided to pray for myself to receive the gift of the Holy Ghost. And sure enough, I began speaking in tongues! I want to encourage you because you can actually try to do this yourself in prayer too. I have a ton of resources for you, which I will share how to access below.

So what exactly is the 1 Hour Prayer Challenge...

The 1 Hour Prayer Time is you spending your first hour of the day with God. Included in that 1 hour of time, is worshipping God in song; praying in your natural language, but the superpower is praying in your heavenly language; meditating and praying on your weekly scripture; getting quiet to hear what the Holy Spirit says to you; and then journaling (writing down) what He says!! Yes I know that will take longer than 5 minutes but you start with 5 minutes, even if you take 1 minute to do those 5 things!

The way the challenge will work is that for the next 7 weeks, you will receive weekly instructions with your prayer time goal for that week. By starting off small, this will help you navigate the challenge week-by-week, plus you will be creating a lifestyle of prayer that lasts.

To help you keep yourself accountable, your first step is to join the 1 Hour Prayer Challenge Facebook Group/Text Community (601-299-4398) so that you can be in community with other like-minded people and more importantly, so you can post your accountability that you prayed each day, in the group. I mean, what's a challenge if no one holds you accountable, right? Exactly!

In this challenge, you will be disciplined to grow spiritually in the areas of prayer, fasting, and giving. The Bible says, WHEN you pray, WHEN you fast, and WHEN you give. That means we are to be doing all three of these things as a lifestyle. Matthew 6 totally backs me up on this!

So let's talk about these 3 areas: FASTING, GIVING, and PRAYING IN THE SPIRIT.

FASTING

Now, one of the things that I want you to add once you get going in the challenge is a 3-day fast! I don't want to tell you which week to add it, but I would say around week 4. The 3-day fast will deepen your intimacy with Holy Spirit and you will hear God even more clearly! Breakthroughs will happen!!

The 3-day fast instructions are simple: For 3 straight days during the week of your choice, you will abstain or deny yourself food from 6 a.m. - 6 p.m., and drink water only! No other liquids during the fasting time. Pure Water. During the time where you feel the urge to snack or eat, you will read (or chew) on scripture! Don't tell anyone you are fasting. It's between you and God. What you do in private, God will reward publicly. Be sure to use the journal to document everything you hear from God during this time.

GIVING

You will also want to pick one day during the fast to give alms to the poor, widowed, or orphaned. It's been said that this is often a missing element of getting a breakthrough, when fasting. We are the hands and feet of Jesus, and there will always be poor among us. It is important for us to be led by Holy Spirit on who to give to during this time. Bottom line: Choose a day to give alms while you're fasting.

If you help the poor, you are lending to the Lord — and he will repay you. Proverbs 19:17

PRAYING IN THE SPIRIT

There are resources at the end of this book to help you grow and learn more about praying in the Spirit. When I received the baptism of the Holy Spirit with evidence of speaking in tongues, it changed the game for me! It deepened my relationship with God completely! So be sure to check those out before you get started!

If you ever have any questions, need prayer, or help for anything, don't hesitate to ask. We are here to help you with this new habit you are forming. You are about to change your life and build a lifestyle of prayer, fasting, giving, and most importantly, a closer intimate relationship with our Lord and Savior, Jesus Christ.

Now be sure you get to bed on time... so that you can be ready to start the challenge tomorrow (or after you have read the resources)!!

Hearts & Hugs

Fon

Please note: This challenge has been run several times and members of the FB group may not be actively going through the challenge with you, but having community support is the whole purpose for joining the group! Plus I'm in there as well. There are units that correspond to each week and you can feel free to post that you prayed in those weekly units (or feel free to just free-post that you prayed). I definitely don't want to make the accountability portion of the challenge too hard, but I want to stress that accountability is the key that unlocks discipline's door.

You may also choose to be accountable to the 1 Hour Prayer Challenge by joining our Text Community and posting your progress there. To join, simply text the words "Prayer Challenge" to 601-299-4398. Each day, you will simply text that you prayed for the specified time.

WEEK ONE

Welcome to Week 1 of the 1 Hour Prayer Challenge!! This week (for the next 7 days including weekends) you will spend 5 minutes in prayer (set alarm for 5:55 a.m. daily). Yup, that's it. Easy enough right?

In that 5 minutes, you will worship with a praise song, read this week's scripture, and then pray in the Spirit for 5 minutes (you can always pray longer of course). After your prayer time, post in the Facebook Group/Text Community (601-299-4398) for accountability by 6:30 a.m. (your time zone) to show that you prayed each day of this week. Feel free to share any testimonies, struggles, or questions that you may have in your post as you progress through the challenge. The FB Community is there to encourage and support you on this amazing journey! I can't wait to see your post in the FB Group!

This week's Scripture to meditate on is Jude 1:20. Feel free to search the scripture in your YouVersion Bible app for different translations to see which translation really speaks to you personally.

But you, dear friends, must build each other up in your most holy faith, pray in the power of the Holy Spirit.

~ Jude 1:20

Now before you get too far into the week, I want to share some tips with you that helped me do this challenge with success! Check them out!

Tips:

* Get up out of the bed!!!! That means your feet MUST hit the floor.
* Find a specific spot to pray (i.e. closet, empty bedroom, bathroom, shower, etc.).
* Stay encouraged. Don't let a mess up throw you off. Just get up the next day.
* Go to bed at a reasonable time.
* Set a curfew on your phone (I use my Alexa Echo Dot and have it wake me up to praise and worship music).
* Put the alarm clock on the other side of the room.

* Drink some water when you get up heading to the prayer spot.
* Remind yourself WHY you're doing this!
* Prepare for obstacles. Combat the enemy with the Word!
* Don't focus on looking a certain way. Wake up, potty, wash hands, drink water and get to it!
* Don't let anything distract you from praying. NOTHING!
* Remember that someone is in need of your prayers in the Spirit. Please don't let them down by you lying down.

Hearts & Hugs,

Fon

WEEK 1: DAY 1

What did the Holy Spirit say to you in your conversation with Him this morning?

_____

_____

_____

_____

_____

_____

_____

_____

_____

_____

_____

_____

_____

WEEK 1: DAY 2

What did the Holy Spirit say to you in your conversation with Him this morning?

_____

_____

_____

_____

_____

_____

_____

_____

_____

_____

_____

_____

_____

WEEK 1: DAY 3

What did the Holy Spirit say to you in your conversation
with Him this morning?

_____

_____

_____

_____

_____

_____

_____

_____

_____

_____

_____

_____

WEEK 1: DAY 4

What did the Holy Spirit say to you in your conversation with Him this morning?

_____

_____

_____

_____

_____

_____

_____

_____

_____

_____

_____

_____

_____

WEEK 1: DAY 5

What did the Holy Spirit say to you in your conversation with Him this morning?

_____

_____

_____

_____

_____

_____

_____

_____

_____

_____

_____

_____

_____

WEEK 1: DAY 6

What did the Holy Spirit say to you in your conversation with Him this morning?

_____

_____

_____

_____

_____

_____

_____

_____

_____

_____

_____

_____

_____

WEEK 1: DAY 7

What did the Holy Spirit say to you in your conversation with Him this morning?

WEEK TWO

Heeeeey!

You made it to Week 2 of the 1 Hour Prayer Challenge!!

This week (for the next 7 days) you will **spend 10 minutes in prayer time** (set alarm for 5:50 a.m. daily). You probably already mastered 10 minutes last week didn't you?

This week's Scripture to meditate on is Romans 12:12 . Feel free to search the scripture in your YouVersion Bible app for different translations to see which translation really speaks to you personally.

Rejoice in our confident hope. Be patient in trouble, and keep on praying.

Romans 12:12 NLT

Here's your weekly reminders of how you will spend the first 10 minutes of the day for this entire week:

1. Worship with a praise song, read this week's scripture, and then **pray in the Spirit for 10 minutes** (you can always pray longer of course).

2. After your prayer time, post in the Facebook Group/Text Community (601-299-4398) for accountability by 6:30 a.m. (your time zone) to show that you prayed each day of this week.

3. Feel free to share any testimonies, struggles, or questions that you may have in your post as you progress through the challenge. The FB Community is there to encourage and support you on this amazing journey!

I can't wait to see your post in the FB Group!

Hearts & Hugs

Fon

WEEK 2: DAY 1

What did the Holy Spirit say to you in your conversation with Him this morning?

_____

_____

_____

_____

_____

_____

_____

_____

_____

_____

_____

_____

_____

WEEK 2: DAY 2

*What did the Holy Spirit say to you in your conversation
with Him this morning?*

_____

_____

_____

_____

_____

_____

_____

_____

_____

_____

_____

_____

_____

_____

WEEK 2: DAY 3

What did the Holy Spirit say to you in your conversation with Him this morning?

_____

_____

_____

_____

_____

_____

_____

_____

_____

_____

_____

_____

WEEK 2: DAY 4

What did the Holy Spirit say to you in your conversation with Him this morning?

_____

_____

_____

_____

_____

_____

_____

_____

_____

_____

_____

_____

_____

_____

WEEK 2: DAY 5

*What did the Holy Spirit say to you in your conversation
with Him this morning?*

_____

_____

_____

_____

_____

_____

_____

_____

_____

_____

_____

_____

WEEK 2: DAY 6

What did the Holy Spirit say to you in your conversation with Him this morning?

_____

_____

_____

_____

_____

_____

_____

_____

_____

_____

_____

_____

_____

WEEK 2: DAY 7

What did the Holy Spirit say to you in your conversation with Him this morning?

_____

_____

_____

_____

_____

_____

_____

_____

_____

_____

_____

_____

WEEK THREE

You made it to Week 3 of the 1 Hour Prayer Challenge!!

This week (for the next 7 days) you will **spend 20 minutes in prayer time** (set alarm for 5:40 a.m. daily). Piece of cake to you huh. LOL!

This week's Scripture to meditate on is Ephesians 6:18. Feel free to search the scripture in your YouVersion Bible app for different translations to see which translation really speaks to you personally.

Pray in the Spirit at all times and on every occasion. Stay alert and be persistent in your prayers for all believers everywhere.

Ephesians 6:18 NLT

Here's your weekly reminders of how you will spend the first 20 minutes of the day for this entire week:

1. Worship with a praise song, read this week's scripture, and then **pray in the Spirit for 20 minutes** (you can always pray longer of course).

2. After your prayer time, post in the Facebook Group/Text Community (601-299-4398) for accountability by 6:30 a.m. (your time zone) to show that you prayed each day of this week.

3. Feel free to share any testimonies, struggles, or questions that you may have in your post as you progress through the challenge. The FB Community is there to encourage and support you on this amazing journey!

I can't wait to see your posts in the FB Group for this week! You got this!

Hearts & Hugs

Fon

WEEK 3: DAY 1

What did the Holy Spirit say to you in your conversation with Him this morning?

_____

_____

_____

_____

_____

_____

_____

_____

_____

_____

_____

_____

_____

WEEK 3: DAY 2

*What did the Holy Spirit say to you in your conversation
with Him this morning?*

_____

_____

_____

_____

_____

_____

_____

_____

_____

_____

_____

_____

WEEK 3: DAY 3

What did the Holy Spirit say to you in your conversation with Him this morning?

_____

_____

_____

_____

_____

_____

_____

_____

_____

_____

_____

_____

_____

WEEK 3: DAY 4

What did the Holy Spirit say to you in your conversation with Him this morning?

_____

_____

_____

_____

_____

_____

_____

_____

_____

_____

_____

_____

_____

WEEK 3: DAY 5

What did the Holy Spirit say to you in your conversation with Him this morning?

_____

_____

_____

_____

_____

_____

_____

_____

_____

_____

_____

_____

_____

WEEK 3: DAY 6

What did the Holy Spirit say to you in your conversation with Him this morning?

_____

_____

_____

_____

_____

_____

_____

_____

_____

_____

_____

_____

_____

_____

WEEK 3: DAY 7

What did the Holy Spirit say to you in your conversation with Him this morning?

_____

_____

_____

_____

_____

_____

_____

_____

_____

_____

_____

_____

WEEK FOUR

Yooooo!

Can you believe you made it to Week 4 of the 1 Hour Prayer Challenge?? I can!!

This week (for the next 7 days) you will **spend 30 minutes in prayer time** (set alarm for 5:30 a.m. daily)!! Now you're starting to look forward to your time with God, right?

This week's Scripture to meditate on is James 5:16. Feel free to search the scripture in your YouVersion Bible app for different translations to see which translation really speaks to you personally.

Confess your sins to each other and pray for each other so that you may be healed.

The earnest prayer of a righteous person has great power and produces wonderful results.

James 5:16 NLT

Here's your weekly reminders of how you will spend the first 30 minutes of the day for this entire week:

1. Worship with a praise song, read this week's scripture, and then **pray in the Spirit for 30 minutes** (you can always pray longer of course).

2. After your prayer time, post in the Facebook Group/Text Community (601-299-4398) for accountability by 6:30 a.m. (your time zone) to show that you prayed each day of this week.

3. Feel free to share any testimonies, struggles, or questions that you may have in your post as you progress through the challenge. The FB Community is there to encourage and support you on this amazing journey!

Hey you, your FB posts for this week are about to be lit and I can't wait to read them! Don't leave out a single detail either :-)

Hearts & Hugs

Fon

WEEK 4: DAY 1

What did the Holy Spirit say to you in your conversation with Him this morning?

_____

_____

_____

_____

_____

_____

_____

_____

_____

_____

_____

_____

_____

WEEK 4: DAY 2

*What did the Holy Spirit say to you in your conversation
with Him this morning?*

_____

_____

_____

_____

_____

_____

_____

_____

_____

_____

_____

_____

_____

WEEK 4: DAY 3

What did the Holy Spirit say to you in your conversation with Him this morning?

_____

_____

_____

_____

_____

_____

_____

_____

_____

_____

_____

_____

_____

WEEK 4: DAY 4

What did the Holy Spirit say to you in your conversation with Him this morning?

_____

_____

_____

_____

_____

_____

_____

_____

_____

_____

_____

_____

_____

WEEK 4: DAY 5

What did the Holy Spirit say to you in your conversation with Him this morning?

_____

_____

_____

_____

_____

_____

_____

_____

_____

_____

_____

_____

_____

WEEK 4: DAY 6

What did the Holy Spirit say to you in your conversation with Him this morning?

_____

_____

_____

_____

_____

_____

_____

_____

_____

_____

_____

_____

_____

WEEK 4: DAY 7

What did the Holy Spirit say to you in your conversation with Him this morning?

_____

_____

_____

_____

_____

_____

_____

_____

_____

_____

_____

_____

_____

WEEK FIVE

It is Week 5 of the 1 Hour Prayer Challenge and the scripture for this week is right on time because you're at the 40 minute prayer mark and your body is probably trying to say you can't, but I say... YES YOU CAN!

This week (for the next 7 days) you will **spend 40 minutes in prayer time** (set alarm for 5:20 a.m. daily)!! Tell your body you're in a challenge and you can't stop, and you won't stop!

Keep watch and pray, so that you will not give in to temptation. For the spirit is willing, but the body is weak!"
Matthew 26:41

You already know this week's Scripture to meditate on is Matthew 26:41. Feel free to search the scripture in your YouVersion Bible app for different translations to see which translation really speaks to you personally.

Here's your weekly reminders of how you will spend the first 40 minutes of the day for this entire week:

1. Worship with a praise song, read this week's scripture, and then **pray in the Spirit for 40 minutes** (you can always pray longer of course).

2. After your prayer time, post in the <u>Facebook Group/Text Community (601-299-4398)</u> for accountability by 6:30 a.m. (your time zone) to show that you prayed each day of this week.

3. Feel free to share any testimonies, struggles, or questions that you may have in your post as you progress through the challenge. The FB Community is there to encourage and support you on this amazing journey!

Hang on in there! You totally got this because God is WITH YOU!

Hearts & Hugs

Fon

WEEK 5: DAY 1

What did the Holy Spirit say to you in your conversation with Him this morning?

_____

_____

_____

_____

_____

_____

_____

_____

_____

_____

_____

_____

WEEK 5: DAY 2

What did the Holy Spirit say to you in your conversation with Him this morning?

_____

_____

_____

_____

_____

_____

_____

_____

_____

_____

_____

_____

_____

WEEK 5: DAY 3

What did the Holy Spirit say to you in your conversation with Him this morning?

_____

_____

_____

_____

_____

_____

_____

_____

_____

_____

_____

_____

_____

WEEK 5: DAY 4

What did the Holy Spirit say to you in your conversation with Him this morning?

_____

_____

_____

_____

_____

_____

_____

_____

_____

_____

_____

_____

_____

_____

WEEK 5: DAY 5

What did the Holy Spirit say to you in your conversation with Him this morning?

WEEK 5: DAY 6

*What did the Holy Spirit say to you in your conversation
with Him this morning?*

WEEK 5: DAY 7

What did the Holy Spirit say to you in your conversation with Him this morning?

_____

_____

_____

_____

_____

_____

_____

_____

_____

_____

_____

_____

WEEK SIX

Oh My Goodness!

You are sooooo close!! It is Week 6 of the 1 Hour Prayer Challenge and you are still waking up daily to pray! Way to go!! Your obedience to God and your prayer conversations with Him are so necessary for the Kingdom!

This week (for the next 7 days) you will **spend 50 minutes in prayer time** (set alarm for 5:10 a.m. daily)!! You can see the finish line at this point can't you?

This week's Scripture to meditate on is Daniel 9:21. Feel free to search the scripture in your YouVersion Bible app for different translations to see which translation really speaks to you personally. This scripture is talking about getting visions while praying!! I told you that you would go deeper with God as you committed to this prayer challenge!

As I was praying, Gabriel, whom I had seen in the earlier vision, came swiftly to me at the time of the evening sacrifice.

Daniel 9:21

Here's your weekly reminders of how you will spend the first 50 minutes of the day for this entire week:

1. Worship with a praise song, read this week's scripture, and then **pray in the Spirit for 50 minutes** (you can always pray longer of course).

2. After your prayer time, post in the <u>Facebook Group/Text Community (601-299-4398)</u> for accountability by 6:30 a.m. (your time zone) to show that you prayed each day of this week.

3. Feel free to share any testimonies, struggles, or questions that you may have in your post as you progress through the challenge. The FB Community is there to encourage and support you on this amazing journey!

You are literally one week away from hitting the goal! Please please please....KEEP GOING!! Post in the FB Group to motivate others and yourself! You WILL MAKE IT!!

Hearts & Hugs

Fon

WEEK 6: DAY 1

What did the Holy Spirit say to you in your conversation with Him this morning?

_____

_____

_____

_____

_____

_____

_____

_____

_____

_____

_____

_____

WEEK 6: DAY 2

What did the Holy Spirit say to you in your conversation with Him this morning?

_____

_____

_____

_____

_____

_____

_____

_____

_____

_____

_____

_____

_____

_____

WEEK 6: DAY 3

What did the Holy Spirit say to you in your conversation with Him this morning?

_____

_____

_____

_____

_____

_____

_____

_____

_____

_____

_____

_____

_____

WEEK 6: DAY 4

What did the Holy Spirit say to you in your conversation with Him this morning?

_____

_____

_____

_____

_____

_____

_____

_____

_____

_____

_____

_____

_____

_____

WEEK 6: DAY 5

What did the Holy Spirit say to you in your conversation with Him this morning?

WEEK 6: DAY 6

What did the Holy Spirit say to you in your conversation with Him this morning?

_____

_____

_____

_____

_____

_____

_____

_____

_____

_____

_____

_____

_____

WEEK 6: DAY 7

What did the Holy Spirit say to you in your conversation with Him this morning?

_____

_____

_____

_____

_____

_____

_____

_____

_____

_____

_____

_____

WEEK SEVEN

THIS IS IT! You are literally at the finish line! This is the week you reach the goal of 60 minutes or 1 Hour of time with God! How do you feel? Are you feeling like you're on top of a mountain? God is right there with you beaming and proud of all the time you have been spending with Him early in the morning.

Now let's finish STRONG!

This week (for the next 7 days) you will **spend 60 minutes in prayer time** (set alarm for 5:00 a.m. daily)!!

This week's Scripture to meditate on is Matthew 6:6. It is the perfect scripture to round the last corner of this challenge. What you have been doing in private, our Father God saw it, and you will get a REWARD!!! See for yourself!!

> *But when you pray, go away by yourself, shut the door behind you, and pray to your Father in private. Then your Father, who sees everything, will reward you.*
>
> *Matthew 6:6 NLT*

Here's your weekly reminders of how you will spend the first 60 minutes of the day for this entire week:

1. Worship with a praise song, read this week's scripture, and then **pray in the Spirit for 60 minutes** (you can always pray longer of course).
2. After your prayer time, post in the Facebook Group/Text Community (601-299-4398) for accountability by 6:30 a.m. (your time zone) to show that you prayed each day of this week.
3. Feel free to share any testimonies, struggles, or questions that you may have in your post as you progress through the challenge. The FB Community is there to encourage and support you on this amazing journey!

I am soooooo proud of you as you kick off this week! I can't wait to chat with you in the FB Group as you push to the end of this challenge day-by-day with your posts.

Hearts & Hugs

Fon

WEEK 7: DAY 1

What did the Holy Spirit say to you in your conversation with Him this morning?

_____

_____

_____

_____

_____

_____

_____

_____

_____

_____

_____

_____

WEEK 7: DAY 2

What did the Holy Spirit say to you in your conversation with Him this morning?

_____

_____

_____

_____

_____

_____

_____

_____

_____

_____

_____

_____

_____

WEEK 7: DAY 3

What did the Holy Spirit say to you in your conversation with Him this morning?

_____

_____

_____

_____

_____

_____

_____

_____

_____

_____

_____

_____

_____

WEEK 7: DAY 4

What did the Holy Spirit say to you in your conversation with Him this morning?

WEEK 7: DAY 5

What did the Holy Spirit say to you in your conversation with Him this morning?

_____

_____

_____

_____

_____

_____

_____

_____

_____

_____

_____

_____

WEEK 7: DAY 6

What did the Holy Spirit say to you in your conversation with Him this morning?

_____

_____

_____

_____

_____

_____

_____

_____

_____

_____

_____

_____

_____

WEEK 7: DAY 7

*What did the Holy Spirit say to you in your conversation
with Him this morning?*

_____

_____

_____

_____

_____

_____

_____

_____

_____

_____

_____

_____

_____

WEEK EIGHT

You have made it to the lifestyle-set week for this challenge! I know you're probably like, why are we doing one more week? Well, because I know that you are just as excited to try out your new prayer lifestyle without the "training wheels" (yes these weekly instructions from me have been the training wheels). And I know you're ready to ride with Holy Spirit on your own (so to speak).

So this week, let's see how you do on your own. This final week of 60 minutes of prayer is all YOU!

I know you can do it because you did it last week. So let's get in one more week to set this prayer routine for life!!

Be sure to stay connected in the Facebook Group/Text Community (601-299-4398) for this lifestyle set week! We want to see you there every day!

Hearts & Hugs

Fon

WEEK 8: DAY 1

What did the Holy Spirit say to you in your conversation with Him this morning?

_____

_____

_____

_____

_____

_____

_____

_____

_____

_____

_____

_____

WEEK 8: DAY 2

What did the Holy Spirit say to you in your conversation with Him this morning?

_____

_____

_____

_____

_____

_____

_____

_____

_____

_____

_____

_____

_____

WEEK 8: DAY 3

*What did the Holy Spirit say to you in your conversation
with Him this morning?*

_____

_____

_____

_____

_____

_____

_____

_____

_____

_____

_____

_____

WEEK 8: DAY 4

What did the Holy Spirit say to you in your conversation with Him this morning?

_____

_____

_____

_____

_____

_____

_____

_____

_____

_____

_____

_____

_____

_____

WEEK 8: DAY 5

What did the Holy Spirit say to you in your conversation with Him this morning?

_____

_____

_____

_____

_____

_____

_____

_____

_____

_____

_____

_____

_____

WEEK 8: DAY 6

*What did the Holy Spirit say to you in your conversation
with Him this morning?*

_____

_____

_____

_____

_____

_____

_____

_____

_____

_____

_____

_____

_____

WEEK 8: DAY 7

What did the Holy Spirit say to you in your conversation with Him this morning?

_____

_____

_____

_____

_____

_____

_____

_____

_____

_____

_____

_____

_____

COMPLETION

Congratulations!! You completed the 1 Hour Prayer Challenge! One of the best things I did when I finished the challenge was tell everyone around me! I want to give you the same opportunity! Share this challenge with your family, friends, and loved ones! There is nothing like helping others grow closer to God through our testimonies!!! Revelation 12:11 says:

They conquered him by the blood of the Lamb and by the word of their testimony; Revelation 12:11

Now, here is a real treat for you! I created a graphic for you to share your challenge completion! Once you have arrived here in the book, text me at 601-299-4398 and I will first of all, congratulate you personally and then send you the graphic that you can use on your social media pages. Be sure to include your testimony about this challenge so that others might be encouraged to take the challenge!

Guess what else? We can stay connected through the FB Group, the text community, and I'd love for you to become a subscriber to the On Assignment by God blog and podcast! And please make sure you stick around in the FB Group so that you can help encourage others on their journey as they join the 1 Hour Prayer Challenge.

Hearts & Hugs,

Fon Strong

ADDITIONAL JOURNALING NOTES:

What is the Holy Spirit saying to you?

_____

_____

_____

_____

_____

_____

_____

_____

_____

_____

_____

_____

_____

_____

_____

SCRIPTURAL RESOURCES

Quality vs Quantity: Matthew 26:36-45 (Amplified Bible)

"So you men could not stay awake and keep watch with Me for one hour?"

Jesus Made Prayer a Priority: Luke 6:12 (KJV)

And it came to pass in those days, that he went out into a mountain to pray, and continued all night in prayer to God.

Jesus' Example: Mark 1:35 (Amplified)

Early in the morning, while it was still dark, Jesus got up, left [the house], and went out to a secluded place, and was praying there.

Early Morning Prayer: Psalm 5:3 (AMPC):

In the morning You hear my voice, O Lord; in the morning I prepare [a prayer, a sacrifice] for You and watch and wait [for You to speak to my heart].

Total Transformation: John 16:13-15 (AMPC):

13 But when He, the Spirit of Truth (the Truth-giving Spirit) comes, He will guide you into all the Truth (the whole, full Truth). For He will not speak His own message [on His own authority]; but He will tell whatever He hears [from the Father; He will give the message that has been given to Him], and He will announce and declare to you the things that are to come [that will happen in the future].14 He will honor and glorify Me, because He will take from (receive, draw upon) what is Mine and will reveal (declare, disclose, transmit) it to you.

15 Everything that the Father has is Mine. That is what I meant when I said that He [the Spirit] will take the things that are Mine and will reveal (declare, disclose, transmit) it to you.

2 Corinthians 3:17-18 (KJV)

17 Now the Lord is that Spirit: and where the Spirit of the Lord is, there is liberty. 18 But we all, with open face beholding as in a glass the glory of the Lord, are changed into the same image from glory to glory, even as by the Spirit of the Lord.

The Why - Romans 8:26-27 (KJV)

26 Likewise the Spirit also helpeth our infirmities: for we know not what we should pray for as we ought: but the Spirit itself maketh intercession for us with groanings which cannot be uttered.

27 And he that searcheth the hearts knoweth what is the mind of the Spirit, because he maketh intercession for the saints according to the will of God.

Resources for Speaking In Tongues

Why Tongues? By Kenneth E. Hagin. If you haven't read this book, it is the smallest (goodest) LOL...I know that's not a real word, but it is great!! Download it on Amazon Kindle cloud reader for only 99 cents! Really helped me understand tongues. I didn't understand it at all when I first started the challenge.

How You Can Be Led by the Spirit of God by Kenneth E. Hagin (YouTube Video).

The Apostle Paul wrote and spoke much about the subject of speaking in other tongues, and he apparently practiced what he preached, for he said, "I thank my God, I speak with tongues more than ye all" (1 Cor. 14:18).

The purpose of this particular article is to briefly set forth seven reasons why every Christian should speak in tongues and to help believers see the blessings that can be theirs through daily appropriating the power of the Holy Spirit in their lives.

Seven Reasons Why Every Believer Should Speak in Tongues By Kenneth E. Hagin.

Reason Number One

The Word of God teaches that when we are filled with the Holy Ghost, we speak with other tongues as the Spirit of God gives utterance. Speaking in tongues is an initial evidence, or sign, of the baptism of the Holy Spirit: "And they were all FILLED WITH THE HOLY GHOST, and began to SPEAK WITH OTHER TONGUES, as the Spirit gave them utterance" (Acts 2:4).

Reason Number Two

Paul encouraged the Corinthian Christians to continue the practice of speaking with other tongues in their worship of God. He also encouraged them to speak in tongues in their individual prayer life as a means of spiritual edification, or building up. The Bible says, "He that speaketh in an unknown tongue edifieth himself . . ." (1 Cor. 14:4).

Paul also stated in First Corinthians 14:14, "For if I pray in an unknown tongue, MY SPIRIT PRAYETH, but my understanding is unfruitful." Notice he said, "My spirit prays."

The Amplified Bible reads, "My spirit [by the Holy Spirit within me] prays . . . ." God is a Spirit. When you pray in tongues, your spirit is in direct contact with God, who is a Spirit. When you speak in tongues, you are talking to Him by divine, supernatural means.

Reason Number Three

A third reason people should speak with other tongues is that speaking with tongues keeps us continually aware of the Holy Spirit's indwelling Presence. Not only is speaking with tongues the initial sign or evidence of the Holy Spirit's infilling, but continuing to pray and to worship God in tongues helps us to be ever-conscious of His indwelling Presence. And if you are conscious of the indwelling Presence of the Holy Ghost every day, that is bound to affect the way you think and live.

Reason Number Four

Speaking in tongues eliminates the possibility of selfishness entering our prayer life. For instance, if I pray a prayer out of my own mind and out of my own thinking, it may be unscriptural. It may be selfish.

Paul wrote to the Church at Rome, "We know not what we should pray for as we ought. . ." (Rom. 8:26). He didn't say we didn't know how to pray, because we are instructed to pray to the Father in the Name of the Lord Jesus Christ (John 16:23–24).

But just because I know how to pray doesn't mean that I know what to pray for as I ought. So Paul said, "We know not what we should pray for as we ought: but the Spirit itself [Himself] maketh intercession for us with groanings which cannot be uttered" (Rom. 8:26).

The Holy Ghost is not going to do our praying for us. He is sent to help us pray. Speaking with other tongues is praying as the Spirit gives utterance. It is Spirit-directed praying. And it eliminates the possibility of selfishness in our prayers.

Reason Number Five

A fifth reason believers should speak with tongues is that it helps them learn to trust God more fully. It builds one's faith to speak in tongues. The Bible says, "Building up yourselves on your most holy faith, praying in the Holy Ghost" (Jude 20).

Speaking in tongues stimulates faith and helps us learn how to trust God more fully. For example, faith must be exercised to speak with tongues because the Holy Spirit supernaturally directs the words we speak. You see, we don't know what the next word will be—we have to trust God for that. And trusting God in one area helps us learn to trust Him in another area.

Reason Number Six

A sixth reason every believer should speak in tongues is that it provides a way for you to pray about things that you wouldn't think to pray about or aren't even aware of. We already know that the Holy Spirit helps us pray for particular situations when we don't know how to pray about those situations. In addition, the Holy Spirit, Who knows everything, can pray things through us for things about which our natural mind knows nothing.

Reason Number Seven

A seventh reason why every believer should speak with tongues is found in James 3:8. "But the tongue can no man tame; it is an unruly evil, full of deadly poison," Yielding your tongue to the Holy Spirit to speak with other tongues is a big step toward being able to fully yield all of your members to God; for if you can yield your tongue, you can yield any member of your body to God.

Speaking in tongues is the initial evidence of the infilling of the Holy Spirit. God has given us this wonderful spiritual gift to bless us, edify us, and refresh us throughout our lives on this earth. Let's receive what God has provided and enjoy the benefits of speaking in tongues!

Source: Rhema.org

ABOUT FON STRONG

My name is Fon Strong and I am the founder and CEO of Encouragement Ink International, LLC, where our mission is to encourage the nations through Christ-centered print, mentorship, and apparel.

I write and publish a daily blog and podcast: On Assignment by God; and I am a four-time published author of two Christian Fiction novels, a nonfiction book, *Permission Slips: Getting God's Permission in Love, Work, and Life*; and an eBook, *My Conversations With God, Volume One*.

I pray that you will be encouraged, blessed, and inspired to be ON ASSIGNMENT BY GOD.

In His Will,

Fon

www.ingramcontent.com/pod-product-compliance
Lightning Source LLC
Chambersburg PA
CBHW070819100426
42813CB00033B/3435/J